Social Media Marketing for Beginners 2023

Get more customers and visitors learning social media marketing strategies, creating engagement and managing effective communication

JUDD SHAUN

Copyright © 2023 Judd Shaun

All rights reserved.

Thank you for choosing this book, you can leave a short review on Amazon if you enjoy it, I'd like to read your opinion!

You can also use the following link:
https://www.amazon.com/review/create-review/

This book includes a related free content, you can get it at:

https://bit.ly/3aTOCE2

TABLE OF CONTENT

INTRODUCTION 1

1 SOCIAL ANALYTICS 9

2 SOCIAL CRM 21

3 SOCIAL MEDIA ENGAGEMENT 31

4 SOCIAL OBJECT 51

5 ESSENTIAL SKILLS IN SOCIAL MARKETING 63

CONCLUSION: TIPS FOR SUCCESSFUL SOCIAL MARKETING 75

THANKS 85

REFERENCES 87

OTHER BOOKS BY THE AUTHOR 93

INTRODUCTION

What is social media marketing?
First, let's talk about what social media marketing is. It is defined as a collection of applications, forums, and websites in an online community that allows the creation and sharing of content, information, and contacts. In simple terms, use social media to drive traffic to your website.

There are a variety of social media tools used within the forum, from forums and blogs to social media and wikis. The main role of those who work in social media is to plan and implement marketing campaigns on social media by publishing content, engaging with followers, and evaluating social analytics to analyze success; as well as using ads on social media.

Types of social media marketing
Communication marketing can be a very broad role, given the number of social media platforms available. Each social media platform works differently and attracts different types of content and different target audiences, so your social media marketing strategy should consider this. Here, we provide a rundown of some of the main forums and how to use them, with some tips taken from RMIT

social media tips and open action.

> Facebook

Having a Facebook page is one of the best free ways to use social media marketing. With over 2.7 billion active users, it is the most popular social media platform out there, making it a must-have for any social media marketing strategy.

It's not the only thing Facebook has to offer, though. As well as being able to create a Facebook business page to help improve brand identity, companies can use Facebook ads to bring more people to their page, create promotional posts, and use Facebook as a series of other marketing strategies.

People of all ages use Facebook, which makes it an ideal place to target different audiences. However, the largest number of users is between the ages of 25 and 35. As of 2021, 56% of users are male, creating a positive gap between men and women.

> Instagram

One of the most popular social media platforms is Instagram, which is another great place to advertise your company. Oberlo estimates that 71% of US businesses are currently on Instagram, which shows how popular and successful it is as part of a marketing strategy.

Many companies use Instagram as a kind of catalog of their products, where they share photos that match the beauty of their product, as well as share photos from their customers using their products - this is called 'user-generated content.' Alternatively, companies can use Instagram to raise awareness of their product, hold competitions that gain more followers, and create sponsored posts.

Whether you want to create a fun product narrative on Instagram news, partner with an influential person to guide specific audiences with your products, or spread your product message, Instagram has a huge list of features and tools that can help you.

> YouTube

You may be surprised to find that YouTube has more active monthly users than Instagram, which makes it a great place to find followers. While Instagram is the best place to advertise your product using photos and short content, YouTube can be a great choice when creating long videos.

In addition to making videos on the YouTube channel, companies can pay to advertise on YouTube and use powerful marketing strategies. It is very common for promoters to make sponsored videos when using or talking about a particular product in their videos, so this could be a good opportunity to target a certain number of people.

YouTube Advertising is controlled by Google. To create a YouTube campaign, you will need to set up a Google AdWords account.

Other social media platforms
- LinkedIn. LinkedIn, which specializes in all social media, can help its businesses become more reliable, hire more skilled employees, connect with customers and build a professional online presence.
- TikTok: The fastest-growing social media platform and seemingly most popular with Gen-Z audiences, TikTok can be used to gain fans with strategies such as powerful marketing and posting short educational videos.
- Snapchat: That appeals to a younger audience, Snapchat can be a great way to spread brand awareness, for example, by posting real-time customer news or videos about business operations.
- Pinterest: Pinterest has nearly 500 million users and loves photo content in the same way as Instagram. Customers often shop directly on Pinterest, so it's a great place to advertise products.

Why is social media marketing so effective?
As we discussed at the beginning of this article, more than 50% of the world's population uses social media. In addition, they spend an average of 2 hours and 25 minutes a day on them. These statistics mean that using social media as part of your digital marketing strategy allows you to easily target multiple audiences. By failing to work on social media, you may miss thousands of supporters.

One example of the success of the social media platform is that Vodafone is creating a new product line to attract 16-24-year-old audiences. The Institute of Data and Marketing states that while Vodafone is investing in promotional advertising, its content has been viewed more than 31 million times on social media, and has gone from 0% to 31% awareness. to the intended audience.

What are the benefits of social media marketing?
There are many benefits to social media marketing, but your main goal is to drive product awareness and traffic to your website. This ultimately leads to more followers, more customers and more business success. However, the other benefits of social media marketing should be mentioned, which we will explain below.

- Social media marketing allows businesses to:
- Reach a larger audience at a lower price
- Keep up with rivals
- Sell products and services on the platform
- Identify specific audiences using demographics and hashtags
- Create a sense of community
- Connect directly with fans and provide customer support
- Analyze product feelings

How to get started on social media marketing
There is a lot to learn in the world of social media

marketing, and there are many ideas to consider. To put it bluntly, we will be discussing what a social media marketing strategy is, how to create a strategy, how to organize your content, and how to engage followers.

What is the marketing strategy of the social media platform?

It is one thing to create a few social media accounts, but if you want to take your business to the next level, you need a marketing strategy. This will be your main social media platform, including your content guidelines, what type of content you can post, marketing campaigns, and how you engage with your audience.

How to create a social media marketing strategy

There are a few things you will need to consider before you start working on your social media marketing strategy. IDM has given tips in their open initiative about creating a campaign strategy, and many of these are important in creating a whole strategy. These tips include:

- Consider business principles. What are the main goals of your business and how will your social media strategy help you achieve those goals?
- Consider the goals of the campaign. What are your specific goals for your next campaign?
- Explain the objectives of the social media platform. Do you have specific social media goals that you want to achieve, such as a certain number of followers or a certain level of engagement?
- Decide on the target audience. Who is the audience you targeted on social media and your next campaign? Think about their age, gender, location, interests, attitudes, and the type of content they frequently associate with.
- Choose your channels. Which social media platforms do you want to focus on, and does

each one need a different strategy? Do you want to use any social media platforms for a short-term campaign, or do you want to build long-lasting communities?

Involve your social media followers

Is important to think about whether your content will promote, motivate or motivate your fans to become customers, where they buy your products or services. There are three important things to consider when it comes to attractive fans:

1. Self-disclosure. Your followers should be able to connect with you and your content, and express themselves by commenting, sharing, and features like polls.
2. Make it your own. Your target audience should understand how your product interacts with their lives, and it should be easy to do things like embed video content on their site.
3. The community. Your fans need to be able to chat with each other and share information with their friends. You can promote this type of community by posting content that gives them opportunities to connect.

How to edit your social media content

A lot of work can go into editing your social media content. There are 6 important things to include in your plan:

1. Important themes and messages. Decide on your entire message and think you want your main message to stay that way each day or improve and create a narrative arc.
2. Dates and times. In your calendar, list all the different days and events that may affect the content (for example, Pride or International Women's Day). You may also want to split each

day into different periods, or time zones when working with an international audience. Then you can find the best dates and times to post content.
3. Platforms. If you have your own time zones, you can decide which social network is most appropriate for each location, and what kind of content makes sense for that forum. For example, you can post a blog on Facebook but a product image on Instagram.
4. Type of content. In your program, list the various types of content you will send, from interviews and promotions to videos and articles. Once everything is in front of you, you will be able to see if you have a good balance of different content formats.
5. Copy of a specific post. It can be helpful to arrange the words in your post so that when they are life, it can be a quick and easy process. If you do not write specific words, you can provide feedback on the copy guide, for example, "Preparing for the launch of a new product".
6. Compatible goods. Add any additional resources such as photos, videos, or links to the program, so you can easily access everything you need and be able to share content with other team members.

Top tips for social media content

We will complete the introduction with some of the top tips to consider when posting content on social media as part of your marketing strategy. These include:

- Use numbers and numbers to increase engagement
- Add subtitles or captions to videos to appeal to everyone

- Tell stories using conversations and thought-provoking episodes
- Ask and answer questions using surveys and surveys
- Add links to your posts where appropriate
- Use a mix of media - photos, videos, graphics, gifs

Final thoughts

Rounding up the intro section, it's paramount to understand that social media marketing is one of the most important tools in any marketing strategy, and it is at the forefront of any digital marketing campaign. With such a high number of people on social media at any given time, being able to organize a social media marketing campaign has never been more important.

So, if you want to reach a larger audience that may have a high conversion rate, then a social media marketing campaign is one of the best ways to do this.

1 SOCIAL ANALYTICS

Social media statistics are not about products. It's about people sharing their lives with others they know based on their interests. And they do not want to be disturbed, especially when someone tries to sell them something! This is where social media analysis begins. We will analyze what this important business tool is; what is wrong; why you need to use it; and, how!

The social media platform offers a wide range of consumers who are ready to interact with the product. Social media is a great place for consumers and products to interact with, as long as they remember one thing: a social media platform can give you your first and final product idea, so both need to be positive. Many businesses take a brand-centric focus when they start with their data analysis journey, and that can be risky. Let's see why!

What is Social Media Analytics?

Techopedia describes communication analysis as follows:

"Social media analytics (SMA) refers to the process of gathering information from social networking sites and analyzing that data for business decisions. This process goes beyond normal monitoring or a basic analysis of retweets or 'preferences' to develop a deeper consumer perception of social media." This is an appropriate definition, although we would like to clarify that "social networking sites" include not only Facebook, Twitter, and the like, but also forums and review sites as well as blogs and news stores. Where consumers can share their beliefs, ideas, and feelings online.

Just as the buzzwords lose their meaning over time, many brands lose sight of the importance of social media analysis because at first glance social media comes with a lot of noise. No one has time to filter out results including spam, bots, and trolls to get the best results. Additionally, brands often make the mistake of using social media analysis on a topic once and then calling it right. The internet is always in a state of flux, so there is an ongoing relationship with the data in the analysis of the communication platform to account for the flexibility that exists in the middle.

The ability to interrupt online noise by pursuing a viable market, and competing consumer competence, combined with consistent monitoring to track conversions over time is a hallmark of effective social media analysis. Simply put, if you have modern tools, social media statistics become a wealth of customer information that you will not find elsewhere. Without them though, the social media platform introduces a game of guessing to the ever-changing slog of information without a shared understanding. Building on this, we can expand the definition above to say that social media statistics are a collection of data obtained using multiple strategies from multiple sources against the same internal and external tools.

To illustrate, let's use a word that is often confused with social media statistics.

So-called Missing Synonyms

If social media statistics are local, what tools contribute to travel? And what is their difference? Social Media Intelligence is the closest cousin to social media statistics.

Social intelligence represents a wide range of technological solutions and methods used to monitor social media, including social media and emerging trends.

This wisdom is analyzed and used to create meaningful content and make business decisions in many fields. Social Media Listening is one of the most often confused words with social media statistics. But public listening works on one specific aspect of social media statistics: Learning about your audience. The goal here is to expose what they like, hate, and hate - as opposed to any assumptions you may have. It's about knowing them as human beings, not just hopes.

For example, if you want to know what the people of Boston have to say about pizza, you can find out by using a tool like NetBase Pro. From there, you can look for something similar to create audience segments to make your interaction more personal.

Social Media Monitoring is a second term that is often confused with social media analysis. It is also thought to be similar to public listening, but both are very different. Public vigilance focuses on tracking public audiences being warned about spikes at work that present an opportunity you would not want to miss, or a potential catastrophe you want to avoid. It's about seeing posts like this one at a time to respond and avoid a virus problem:

Social Competitive Analysis is a process of investigating your product's competitors and their audience. Because a social media platform is such a transparent platform, social media analytics tools can be applied to more than your products. This gives you a chance to see how they help their customers, what consumers like or hate about them, and what new products or services they offer. This information allows you to see what your shared audience enjoys, so you can use new ideas that you may not have ever had yourself. Additionally, you can save the day when things go wrong, or save your budget by learning from the mistakes of competitors.

And since consumers' attitudes never stop, brands can also monitor how other brands treat the social situation to adjust when things get closer to home. Earlier this summer Quaker Oats canceled its old Aunt Jemima logo due to concerns about racial impacts on consumers. Others pay attention.

Image Analytics is a new feature that has been made possible by the emergence of social media statistics technology. Image statistics enhance the quality of text analysis by identifying scenes, facial expressions, geographical areas, product logos and more in public images. This is especially helpful if the product has been photographed, but is not explicitly stated in the text.

As social media users become more and more visible, the inability to perform image statistics becomes a hindrance when researching social media analytics tools. If you are a social media analytics tool it does not take pictures of where your product is depicted, but it is not explicitly stated, you are missing out on a lot of conversation. And to make sure you don't miss out on anything, you need to not only capture full logos, but also modified, partially or postponed branding brands.

Social Media Sentiment Analysis

The concept of social media is a compilation that works in all aspects of your social media statistics. Without you, you have no way of figuring out why you suddenly get 500K more "likes" or shares than usual. What if height is too much for you? The only way to find out is to analyze the emotions. This social media mathematical platform uses Natural Language Processing (NLP) to determine whether the public discourse is good or bad, as well as measure the power of those feelings. This helps you evaluate responses so as not to waste energy on irrelevant posts while ignoring posts you make.

Consumer Sentiment

Emotions when talking about dogs in public - "love" is strong. Customer Experience Analytics includes customer and voice-to-customer (VoC) information such as surveys, reviews, website response, chat messages, market research, and data from internal systems such as a help center, help center, and web support collected through CRM tools. This additional data can be brought to your social media analysis to give you a complete understanding of your customers across all contact areas.

And when it comes to consumer understanding, Quid Social is a social media analytics tool that is extremely effective in helping brands do just that.

Complete SMA Guide
➢ Quid Social Ups Ante to Social Media Analytics

Quid Social easily integrates with your analysis of the NetBase social media platform and distributes it as a map, providing relevant social content in an instant. In other words, it is your social media title - displayed. This symbiotic relationship is great because using different data analysis tools or sources is an unnecessary headache that you do not have to deal with to gain practical wisdom in your data.

If your tools are solid, heavy or tedious, then chances are you will miss something between the tools, or because of frustration. Quid Social solves the problems users face when combining their social media analytics from disconnected sources by providing a single solution and action. In other words, the next level of social media analysis tool integrates your data to create a compact and easy-to-understand window in online accounts. In the same way that Quid Pro allows users to analyze corporate data sets, copyrights, or news and blogs, Quid Social uses the same visual interface to delve into any social media topic to extract information from retrieved data to inform decision-makers of your product. This is achieved through the next generation of artificial intelligence (AI) driven by social media databases that provide a 360-degree context of public accountability in any subject. And no matter how good your subject may be, someone is there to talk about it online. Quid Social captures the depth of all social media, consumer reviews, forums and much more - ensures you capture everything.

And not transferring your data from one tool to another saves time and energy, which translates directly into your bottom line. It also provides in-depth community coverage that allows Quid users to make smarter, faster-driven data for their business, surpassing the fullness of analytics tools in the social media platform.

Quid Social allows users to not only analyze social media, but to emerge emerging styles and themes, analyze the stories of a key ideas leader (KOL), analyze and monitor competitors and evaluate the performance of a social media facilitator - to name a few. The insight gained from these areas can increase your balance in the form of speed at which brands can make strategic business decisions; allowing brands to turn around to avoid pitfalls, see the white market area and stay a step ahead of the competition.

Additionally, Quid Social visualizes major public chat drivers that allow you to see connections between small social media conversations nearby. This online news display allows users to quickly understand the angle the target audience is talking about on a topic or issue.

> Quid-Social-highlight-for-social-media-analytics statistics

As one of the basic principles of social media analytics is to discover and meet consumer needs, this ability to detect emerging conversations in response to social or market motives allows products to move faster and enhance voice sharing before other forms get the chance to move.

And all of this gives a bonus of growing a good product idea within the media stream. They say the morning bird gets a worm and that works here; as the leading developers have the opportunity to design, submit, and direct narratives. At that point, the competition plays a catch.

Meeting consumer needs quickly translates directly into a positive community feeling built on consumer love. And since people like to share their product information on social media, brands can directly track these changes as they apply to their social media metrics, and how they relate to the competition. Quid Social not only helps with real-time analysis on any topic but also the ability to continue to monitor product-related discussions; which gives brands more understanding of when their messages need to be changed to have the best impact. Having your social media statistics under one roof allows you to quickly check your campaign message to see what makes sense and what's not.

With public speed these days, the ability to monitor, edit and apply your product message quickly transforms the game of your social media marketing team. Additionally, this information can be used to identify competitive areas focused on innovation and R&D. They also provide an in-depth insight into how consumers feel or react to market trends, innovations and competitive products relevant to your industry.

Quid Social also covers the breadth and depth of any topic with social media coverage covering more than 200 countries, large and small mining channels for social media 27 months of history and forward data. The spread of social media history, as well as real-time analysis of any online chat - anytime and anywhere you need it. Below are some of the social media details and analytical functionality available from Quid Social:

- Powerful network views to detect emerging trends, topics and patterns in data
- Scatterplot, bar graph, histogram and timeline view
- Improved integration of short text with auto-composing and summary collections
- Document and emotional level aspect
- Feedback from people, company and business environment

- Public participation counts
- Author knowledge and people knowledge
- Wide filter and tagging power
- Color options with custom view data images
- The x / y axis parameters are customized for detailed graph details

Simply put, how your product can twist, extract and show your social media articles end up presenting a unique way of appearing in social media analysis.

> Quid-Social-Timeline-View-Social-Media-Analytics

But the digging of the market communication forum, competition and consumer intelligence is still part of the battle. What you do with that information is take it all the way.

The Way is Everything

The best investment you can make is in social media analytics tools that bring all of the above operations into one place. This gives you a glimpse behind the curtain - and you're smart to do it by watching and listening and reading, not pushing your agenda.

Imagine having a VIP ticket to the show - it doesn't get you on stage singing with celebrities unless you build a relationship with them later. Once they see that you care enough to come to the whole show you may be drawn to join them. This is the best way to promote interaction between your product and your audience. That's how you make friends on social media.

Use Case for Social Media Analytics

Of course, it's not just about making friends or engaging your audience - though that is an important marketing effort. There are many ways to test the data provided by the data. It is like peeling an orange to get a fruit that is split in half. In other words, the information obtained through social media analysis can empower every aspect of a product's operations. Here are some examples:

Increase Customer Acquisition

Your customers are the lifeblood of your product. Careful management of their journey from early awareness to well-known customers through social media statistics is essential for your maintenance, as well as the long life of your product. Consistent communication with your customers is important, such as building a history of their presence with new inventions when new needs arise. For example, Activision saw its product grow by delivering what it knew its audience wanted. Their Overwatch League garnered more than 10M views in its first week, as well as more than 200K per session. Recently, Amtrak saw an opportunity during the violence to make major changes, bringing tools and information to make their customers feel safer as they travel the railways.

Protect Product Health

A brand is a collection of all the contact and interaction areas consumers have with the product, in addition to messages coming directly from the company. Finally, the consumer has the key to seeing the product through products that constantly strive to influence the positive feeling of the consumer. Seeing a product affects many things, the biggest impact being your balance sheet.

Smart brands make a move based on social media statistics to push consumer sentiment into a vibrant and vibrant product life in the system. Following the outbreak of the COVID-19 epidemic, Chick-fil-A responded quickly by donating $ 10.8 million in relief efforts to the coronavirus. And when the riots broke out earlier this year, they rushed to the ballpark to reach out to their customers on social media, letting them know they cared. It is a quick and immersive act like this that captures the love of consumers all the time.

Low Cost of Cost of Customer Care

Customer care takes a lot of dedicated attention, and these days customer care is a 'permanent' situation. Consumers have no hesitation in reaching out to brands when problems arise, and they are waiting for answers. Consistent analysis of the social media platform helps brands integrate complex pieces of consumer needs to inform innovation to address common issues more economically. Westin overrides eligibility complaints in response to consumer "wishes". Provide "health" professionals to guide their self-esteem while staying in a hotel, and sign an agreement with Peloton to provide their guests with group cycling.

Increase Product Delivery

Social media statistics help companies get into emerging trends by informing them of the products and services demanded by consumers. Additionally, the effective information produced helps to identify market opportunities thus reducing risk to ensure the successful launch of your product.

Increase Campaign Performance

Social media statistics allow brands to learn more effectively what their audience cares about and what influences their purchasing decisions. This information allows marketing departments to build a personal and consistent marketing experience. The potential here for products is enormous with the added benefit of real-time response that allows for mid-campaign optimization. How brands put social media statistics to work are limited to art. For example, through clever promoters, iHeartRadio has produced great collaborations at the iHeartRadio Awards and nominated artists.

By creating thoughtful and attractive marketing strategies, brands can create sensitive customer engagement that enhances campaign performance - just ask the city of

Las Vegas.

Improve Disaster Management

How social media statistics can guide brands in the event of a crisis should be the amount of acceptance alone of the cost-saved response rate. The severity of the disaster and the length of time it expires, or less noticeably, can have serious consequences for companies that can last for years. Their sudden nature points to the need to analyze the media platform to help fulfill your disaster risk management response goals.

Last year when Zion Williamson blew up one of his Nikes at the Duke-UNC game on national television, it was hard to shake Nike if they did not move forward with the online narrative. Everyone saw it in real-time and they entered social media like wildfire. Fortunately, Nike came ahead of him immediately, and he successfully directed the conversation. Also, check out how James Madison University uses Social Monitoring to understand social misunderstandings and to gauge when, if and how, potential problems - among other things.

Sow Wisely and Reap the Reward

Many tools offer some of the features listed above, and when budgeting, starting there is better than completely ignoring social media statistics. Ultimately, though, you want to invest in a set of tools that do all of the above, with a commitment to innovation in the event of the next technological breakthrough. And a history of doing that before. The more data you get, the better your understanding of your audience, and the better you can give them as they wish. That's what gets them back on track. And that's what analytics platform analytics does for brands.

2 SOCIAL CRM

What is Social CRM?

There is a change taking place in the way the business is done. Traditional forms of marketing and sales are gradually abandoned to adopt a growing form of social media. New business models have been created in this rapidly evolving marketplace and businesses must stay on top of this unique perspective. Social CRM's latest developments in customer relationship management tools. This field can be used internally, externally, or in a combination of both. Therefore, it can help the customer community and promote sales, or it can help facilitate communication between the company's business units.

Public Customer Relationship Management is one of the most effective and efficient ways for businesses to communicate with customers through various social media platforms such as LinkedIn and Facebook. Community Customer Relationship Management integrates social media platforms with the Customer Relationship Management (CRM) system to provide insight into customer-product interaction, and to improve customer interaction quality. In short, the integration of CRM and social media is a unique way for businesses to establish customer relationships through a variety of tools on social media.

Shift in Focus

Public CRM takes the CRM tool one step further by allowing real-time data exchange. Like news feeds on social media, robust updates allow for more accurate analysis. Allows the use of the social media platform to communicate with customers in a closely monitored community. This is otherwise known as monitoring social media. With tough competition across all markets, the focus has shifted to customer information. Analytical engines and decisions are needed in managing a large network of social media. The marketplace has been replaced by customer interaction and the goal is to improve relationships through meaningful and more personal communication.

Consumer Community

Traditional marketing has always been a one-way discussion. Whether it is a TV ad, an ad, or a radio broadcast, advertising speaks to the customer, not to him. There has never been a quick forum for a consumer to respond so far. This can have a positive or negative impact depending on how the company diverses the CRM practice. What businesses should be aware of is that communities will emerge from almost every product, no matter where they intervene. Therefore, it is in their best interest to get involved and have a say in that forum as soon as possible. With a good idea, marketing teams are now able to work with like-minded people in a shared space, the ultimate agenda is transformation.

Socializing is Cheap

The most common way a CRM platform is used for data analysis. Strategic, customer-based decision-making is now driven by real-time reporting, monitoring and statistics. With flexible trackings such as customer behavior, keywords and click-through, businesses can determine features such as the best shipping time and which products are popular. They can use this data to drive revenue. Although sometimes frustrating, this modern marketing component is more expensive compared to the conventional model. The program evaluates customer interaction, ideas and communication across the community. This information is then used to drive product, marketing and sales strategies.

Collaborative collaboration
Businesses with internal CRM forums also benefit from public opinion. Internal social CRM facilitates communication and collaboration across all business units and allows for a customer-focused sales cycle. With internal news feeds, ropes and the ability to "follow" or "love" colleagues, transparency among the remnants of the organization has never been greater. Having an open server between product, support and sales allow you to streamline business processes more than ever before.

What to Look For
The best public CRMs on the market help ensure the low cost of customer acquisition and maintenance through various analytics processes. They help companies make informed decisions throughout the sales cycle from leading production to improving conversion costs. This is based on the related success of their various social media campaigns. Large companies can marry and analyze large amounts of data in public statistics to analyze customer interaction in real-time reporting. Ultimately, a good social CRM will provide decision support to drive growth through custom, targeted advertising.

The general takeaway is that the advent of technology is inevitable and is growing exponentially. In other words, do not miss the train. Consumers are the driving force behind the modern-day market. They have a bigger voice than before and businesses are at greater risk of being ignored or blacklisted, based on customer perceptions. The first problem companies face is the stubbornness and error of the user. It creates an unnecessary upside when the whole company resists adopting a new business model but ultimately will not have a choice. Social CRM is the future of customer management and what better way to lead to success, than with a consumer voice in your pocket?

Traditional V / S Social CRM

Traditional CRM is very different from the social CRM system. Traditional CRM primarily stores and manages important customer information such as names, company details, location, transaction history and more. Custom CRM downloads customer information, especially in email and phone conversations, company records or customer-provided data on surveys or feedback forms. On the other hand, Social CRM tools offer better advantages compared to traditional CRM as they download customer information through social networking sites such as LinkedIn and Facebook which help businesses in providing the best customer service in the form of aggressive marketing. domain now.

The world of marketing and marketing has seen many changes in recent times. The power of the sales and marketing domain changes rapidly. To balance the pace of these common changes and to be informed of new and advanced marketing strategies and marketing strategies businesses need to stay on their toes at all times. Gone are the days when consumers were accustomed to buying products and services based on the names of sales and marketing professionals. With the advent of the internet, power has changed dramatically and consumers are smarter now. They go to many websites, and check out reviews and feedback on products and services they are looking forward to buying.

They also check and ask their community members about the products and services they need to buy and then make any purchase decision. In these cases, Social Customer Relationship CRM serves as a joy to sell with marketing professionals to identify clients effectively and in a personal way. This is because social CRM software is not just based on customer information but is built on the type of conversation consumers have with the business on various social media platforms. This helps sales professionals and marketers build stronger and stronger relationships with consumers. On the other hand, Traditional CRM is based on targeted advertising to gather customer information to target campaigns to specific audiences and aims to retain existing customers.

Customer Relationship Management helps sales and marketing professionals create a better way for consumers, provides faster and more advanced customer service through a preferred customer communication platform, and empowers customers to share their knowledge with billions of people online.

CRM Tool for social media & Strategies

As we know customer interaction is a major source of Community Customer Relationship Management System, so it is based on the following operations metrics to analyze the level of successful customer interaction.

➢ Type of followers

Social Customer Relationship CRM also provides a detailed view of the number of followers and lets businesses know how many are following social media platforms and engaging with their content.

➢ Total Traffic

CRM communication software calculates the total amount of traffic and conversion rates that occur through social networking sites. This statistic helps businesses determine how many customers visit their website and how many of them click and convert to customer service.

➢ Customer Engagement

The public CRM system not only counts the number of

clicks and traffic measurements on a website but also provides a detailed picture of customer engagement that takes place through interviews.

> Product Visibility

CRM communication is also very helpful in checking how many followers are talking about a company or product, and when those customers and visitors share their knowledge through social media.

Differences between Social CRM & social media

Social media is nothing but a combination of various social media platforms that include various social networking sites such as Facebook, Twitter, and LinkedIn. These various social networking sites are used by consumers to express their views on specific products or services they have used and to share their positive and negative feedback on these sites. On the other hand, Social CRM software enables businesses to know what customers are talking about on social media of any kind or business, helping businesses meet customer needs effectively and in a personal way.

Power of Community CRM

The power of social CRM is undeniable and overlooked as it is based on the power of social cohesion and collaboration. These two aspects are common in social media and play an important role in communication strategy. Of course, there is indeed a certain inevitable danger when public participation is invited. Businesses cannot always control what consumers say in any way on any social media platform. But yes, businesses can keep track of consumer postings and feedback. Businesses can respond to customer feedback and respond to it, and engage with them in a positive way that encourages constructive dialogue. With the help of CRM software for social media, businesses can analyze customer reviews, feedback, concerns, complaints, and needs and create innovative and effective ways to participate in customer conversations.

Another feature of this type of CRM that benefits businesses are that it gives businesses the ability to track the latest trends in the market and provide a detailed view of what consumers are saying about their business or any other company. It enables businesses to know how consumers feel about specific business products and services that allow businesses to meet customer needs and pain points effectively. This CRM enables businesses to receive early warning of any negative feedback given to consumers on social media. This helps businesses deal with consumer pain at the beginning of dissatisfaction. It allows the business to diminish if any damage to the corporate environment has occurred in the first place. Therefore, it also provides a unique platform where businesses can address consumer concerns quickly and effectively.

As we know, any negative feedback can enter the modern era and can tarnish the overall image of the company but with the help of social CRM, businesses can deal with dissatisfied customers right away.

In addition to controlling negative feedback and dealing with business pain points, consumers with the support of this CRM can also produce and disperse useful content related to their products and services. It also utilizes the power of a variety of tools that allow businesses to track customer responses and reviews and be able to identify a highly influential customer who spreads positive words about your company and other people looking to him for information and guidance. When businesses receive information about these important influences, they can reward them which leads to the company's interest.

Benefits of Social CRM

Social Customer Relationship CRM is personal and unique in communicating effectively with consumers. Includes community CRM as the middle part of the business can create surprises and discounts. The main advantages are the following:

Customer Retention

As we know customer loyalty in any business improves when customer questions are resolved quickly. On the same note, this CRM offers great benefits to businesses when it comes to keeping customers long-term. It allows businesses to deal with customer problems, challenges and complaints quickly and effectively. This approach leads to the development of a level of confidence in customer perceptions. In addition to solving problems the public customer relationship management tool also enables businesses to know how their customers feel about their products and services and businesses also know the lifestyle of their customers and the purchasing interests that help them to craft and manage products and services as they say. customer needs and preferences. The public customer relationship management tool allows businesses to develop social media strategies that enable them to communicate effectively with consumers. This is a way to make the consumer feel lucky because he feels happy when asked about his suggestions for making products and services better. So by doing all these businesses make sure their customers are loyal to them and encourage them to spread the word of encouragement.

A Quick Leading Generation

Another benefit of CRM Social media software is the fast-moving generation that helps businesses grow sales. It empowers businesses to upload relevant content to social media platforms that address consumer needs, and critical points, and encourage consumers to reap the rewards of products and services that lead to faster-leading production. Apart from this, good word of mouth and reviews for your existing customers posted on social media encourages friends and family to trust your products and services and lead to increased ROI.

Strong brand presence

Undoubtedly CRM and social media integration are the most effective and personal ways for businesses to communicate with consumers. It offers many business opportunities today to mark its global presence. To improve the product presentation of the business, these forums play an important role. The contribution of the Public Customer Relationship Management Tool to modern marketing and marketing strategies is truly unique as it gives businesses a platform to showcase their products and services in a way that appeals to the consumer directly.

This CRM utilizes the power of customer interaction and discussions that take place on social media portals. These business and consumer group discussions catalyze to make the presence of any product stronger. With the help of social CRM software, many tasks can be created that can improve the product presence of any business effectively. For example, an entity may promote content that incorporates features of the products and services it provides in the form of awareness-related blogs or how its products and services can be useful to its customers.

Posting these business blogs can encourage more consumer engagement. Consumers can find important information about products and services and can also comment on blogs that generate customer engagement as well. Businesses can also post their web blog links to their social media portfolios inviting more customer engagement and thus enhancing product presence. In addition to these processes, a business can also identify the main promoter who spreads positive messages about their business and can reward that motivator. This action creates a level of confidence in the minds of the customers and they feel special because their response is not only audible but also practical.

Reduce support costs

For any customer, it is very annoying to drive and wait for IVR for long minutes by asking a simple question or registering a complaint. This annoys the customer and causes them more dissatisfaction. However social media offers great help for customers where they can discuss their problems and businesses can deal directly with customers and their problems in a better personal way. This method saves a lot of your time for both the customer and the business and is effective in reducing business support costs. Therefore, this CRM works to guide leaders, transform them into customers and improve global product presence. Any business today, no matter how small, medium or large, can choose a tool for managing Community customer relationships to chart the road to success. The power of CRM and the integration of the communication platform dramatically changes the flexibility of the marketing and marketing environment where content and customer engagement play an important role and ensure improvement in business growth.

The reason for its success and why businesses like to use it in their business process is because this CRM provides businesses with a way that encourages them to educate consumers about their content and not pressure them to buy. Consumer education regularly enhances the sense of trust among consumers leading to faster customer acquisition and better sales.

Better Lead Changes

Community CRM tools also provide a great way to improve lead conversion. As a better understanding of consumer interests and needs is acquired by marketing and sales professionals, it improves the chances of lead conversion dramatically.

3 SOCIAL MEDIA ENGAGEMENT

What is social media?

A social network is an interactive forum in which content is created, distributed and shared individually on the web. Scholars Andreas Kaplan and Michael Haenlein of ESCP European Business School describe the social media platform as "a group of online applications that build on Web 2.0 ideas and technologies, and that allows for the creation and exchange of user-generated content." Social networking websites and apps allow users to create and exchange user-generated content when people talk, share information, participate and interact with technologies such as blogs and social networking sites. Over the past decade, social media has become one of the most powerful sources of news updates, online interaction, networking, viral marketing and entertainment.

Communication Features

Before the name Web, 2.0 was introduced in 1999, web pages featured graphic content such as text and images. Websites running Web 1.0 technologies, where webmasters and owners were not the main content providers. The information on the Internet is aimed at inactive audiences who have received rather than provided content. However, with the introduction of Web 2.0 internet technology in the early 21st century, social networking sites such as blogs began to allow users to interact and interact with each other in visual communities. This more open, integrated approach to social media communication is very similar to the upward trend that reflects the early years of the web.

The social media platform began to integrate the features of Web 2.0 websites, providing rich user experience, flexible content, rating, openness, and integrated intelligence. Active social media users can take advantage of a variety of features that allow them to 'like,' create and post photos and upload videos and text. Users can then share this information, either with a selected group of friends or publicly across the web. However, this also opened up social media websites to make spam, trick and burn by unscrupulous or immature users. However, the social media platform has grown rapidly in the U.S. and globally because of its mix of technology and social media to build value together.

Types of Communication

Some of the current most popular types of social media are social networking sites such as Facebook, which had more than a billion active users per month in October 2012. Several types of online platforms are categorized under a huge social media umbrella. These categories include:

- Social Networking: Social networking websites allow users to create web pages that contain personal portfolios and interests. These pages are used to connect with friends, colleagues and other users to share media, content and communication. Examples of social media platforms include Facebook, LinkedIn, Myspace and Bebo.
- Visual social media platforms are becoming more and more popular, with Instagram surpassing Twitter in the number of its users.

Data has shown that a tweet covering a picture has a 150% chance of sharing. There are also new networks like Snapchat, which are slowly growing in popularity, especially among younger generations.

- Web blogs: One of the oldest and most popular forms of social media blogging. Blogs are often viewed as online journals ordering content in chronological order, or by day, month, year and category. Users can also keep "vlogs," or video blogs, with shared or homemade videos. Blogging websites include WordPress, Blogger and Tumblr.
- Microblogs: Microblogs are blogging tools that include short posts, unlike journal-style posts. Users are often limited to posting a few lines of text, or uploading individual photos and videos. Microblogging is more likely to post instant updates and distribute content on mobile devices. Notable microblogging sites include Twitter and Tumblr. However, social networking sites such as Facebook, LinkedIn, and Myspace also have their microblogging features.
- Content Communities: Users in content communities organize, share and comment on different types of content, including photos and videos. YouTube, Flickr and Scribd are examples of content communities.
- Wikis: Wiki websites allow the public community to add and edit content to a community-based website. One of the most popular wikis is Wikipedia.
- Podcasts: Podcasts of audio and video files available through subscription services such as Apple iTunes. The term "podcast" is a neologism derived from "broadcast" and "pod"

(as in "iPod"), as Podcasts are often heard on portable media players.

Other types of social media include the following:
- Ratings and reviews sites (e.g. Yelp)
- Social bookmarking or public tagging features (e.g. Digg; Stumble Upon)
- Forums and discussion boards
- Visible social worlds (e.g. Second Life, World of Warcraft)
- Music and audio sharing (e.g. Spotify; Pandora Radio)

Social media can also be categorized by its ability to facilitate specific community activities. These social functions usually include ownership, dialogue, sharing, presence, relationships, dignity, and groups. Kaplan and Haenlein developed a segmentation system using six different types of social media platforms - collaboration projects (e.g. Wikipedia), blogs and microblogs (e.g. Twitter), content communities (e.g. YouTube), sites social media (e.g. Facebook), visual game worlds (e.g. World of Warcraft), and virtual social worlds (e.g. Second Life).

Social Media Marketing Communications

The social media platform serves as an inexpensive communication channel to promote brands to a targeted audience.

Media Communication and Integrated Marketing Communication

Some popular tweets have been posted by companies and businesses. Powerful brands like Coca-Cola and McDonald's boast about Facebook pages with millions of followers. Social media, including social media, makes it very important for companies to ensure their online exposure is directly linked to product image and message. Along with television, radio, and printing, the communications platform is part of a comprehensive communication ecosystem to create something fun and seamless for consumers on multiple channels. Similarly, integrated marketing communications are increasingly embedding a platform for communication in the advertising mix to reach consumers across the web and mobile devices. Facebook Business Page: Social networking sites such as Facebook can serve as manufacturers leading social media marketing campaigns.

Product authentication

The explosion of social networking websites has led to an important trend in social media marketing. Social media marketing programs often focus on efforts to create content that attracts attention and encourages readers to share it on social media. The message of the production company still spreads from user to user and it sounds audible again because it seems to come from a reliable, third-party source against the product or the company itself. Social networking sites and blogs allow people to retweet or re-post comments written by a product creator. When that person repeats the message, the contacts can see it, which means the message reaches more people. Because of the dangers of social media, companies often use social networking sites to promote products and services orally. As product information is distributed and replicated across the social network, more traffic is brought to the company's website. This results in the acquired media instead of paid media and both act as leading producers and create a good brand reputation.

Consumer Intelligence

The social network allows advertisers to adjust their segmentation strategy by reaching a targeted target audience. For example, Pinterest, a social bookmarking site with a large number of female users, attracts women-focused companies.

Social networking sites also reveal a wealth of

information about potential interests in products and services. Today, new semantic analytics technology allows advertisers to find buy signals based on shared and online content. Understanding these signs can help marketing professionals understand potential opportunities and help advertisers run less targeted campaigns.

Engagement Advertising and PR

The business forum allows anyone and everyone to express an idea or opinion somewhere in the way of a marketing company. With social networking sites, brands can have conversations and interactions with individual fans. These personal connections can deepen and strengthen product loyalty between potential customers and potential customers. Thus, each customer who participates illegally becomes part of the marketing department, as some customers read their comments or reviews.

Facebook and other social media platforms are often used to tune customer conversations and quickly signal customer service problems and concerns. However, these conversations can also be replicated on other social media platforms and channels. Products often use a social media platform to turn customer comments and testimonials into compelling content for personal marketing, advertising, and other marketing strategies. Listening to the "conversation" of a social media platform helps companies keep abreast of public sentiments about their product. By tracking and analyzing discussions on social media, social media professionals can catch problems early and prevent negative disclosures from turning into full-blown problems.

This communication process is critical to the successful integration of the communication platform into the company's marketing communications strategy. Organizations can use the social media platform to enhance communication at a lower cost across all promotional mixes, promote product awareness, and generally, improve customer service.

Digital Marketing Characters

Digital marketing uses Internet-connected devices to engage consumers with online advertising, especially through pull-and-drop methods.

Digital marketing is defined as the use of online devices such as computers, tablets, smartphones, and game consoles to engage consumers with online advertising. One of the key principles of digital marketing is to create simple, seamless, and user-friendly user information for targeted audiences. In addition, eliminating the amount of consumer effort required to create digital content helps to establish a continuous, automated relationship between products and their audience. Blog website: Digital advertisers often include blogs and other social media features on their corporate websites to promote web traffic.

Pull Digital Marketing

Pull digital marketing is characterized by consumers looking for marketing content. Consumers may use tactics that include search engines, email newsletters, text messages, or web feeds to search for product information. Push technologies deliver content as it is more accessible and targeted at the customer census. However, microtargeting tends to produce smaller audiences and leads to higher creation and distribution costs.

Websites, blogs, and streaming media (audio and video) are examples of attracting digital marketing. In all of these channels, users should navigate to the website to view the content. It is up to consumers to create digital content - text, images, videos, and audio - that is important and attractive enough to attract web visitors, increase page visibility, and improve search engine rankings.

Building online communities on related social networking sites such as Facebook and YouTube is another attraction used by brands to increase the number of interactions with prospects and customers. Companies often use their corporate websites and blogs to build authority and credibility in their field, as well as to improve their search engine rankings. Major search engines such as Google often target sites based on the quality and relevance of their content. Therefore, if the product is high quality on Google, it is likely that web users will find their website.

Push Digital Marketing

Push digital marketing occurs when advertisers send messages with the consent of recipients with or without permission. These digital marketing strategies include advertising on websites and blogs. Email, text messaging, and web feeds are also considered push digital marketing where the recipient has not agreed to receive the marketing message. This practice is also known as spam. The opposite is spam marketing, which uses pre-licensed recipient technology. Vendors obtain a consumer permit to send a registered subscription or written consent.

Subscriptions offer the opportunity to compress content for fans and followers, prompting them to visit the product video channel, social media page, or business website. Media and video media releases can be easily distributed through online distribution services. Journalists, bloggers, and other content producers visit these sites to get news. Products can receive web traffic from media publications and blogs that use their news releases as sources.

Other Types of Digital Marketing

The company may not only use digital marketing or advertising strategies, or may not use these strategies at all. Other marketing strategies can include a variety of advertising or pullbacks. For example, multi-channel communication uses technology to push and pull messages simultaneously.

Types of Online Advertising

Types of online advertising include a banner, semantic,

affiliate, social networking, and mobile.

One of the great benefits of online advertising is the rapid publication of unlimited information by places or time constraints. Online advertisers can customize ads, making consumer targeting more efficient and clearer. For example, AdWords, Yahoo! Search Marketing, and Google AdSense enable ads to be displayed on related web pages or next to related search results. On the other hand, consumers have more control over the content they see, which affects the timing, placement, and visibility of online ads. Within the realm of online marketing, online advertising includes display advertising, affiliate marketing, search engine marketing (SEM), and mobile advertising.

Banner ad: Banner ads are examples of online advertising.

Show Advertising

Advertising is the use of web ads or advertisements placed on a third-party website or blog to drive traffic to a business website and increase brand awareness. These banners contain vertical or animated images, as well as interactive media that combine audio and video. Display of advertising uses location and location redirecting - scanning user cookies and browser history to determine demographics, location, and interests - to target relevant ads to those browsers.

In addition to contextual guidance, online advertising is focused on online user behavior. This practice is known as moral discipline. For example, if a user is known to have recently visited many automotive websites based on clickstream-enabled cookies stored on a user's computer, that user may be offered ads automatically when they visit other non-automated sites. Semantic analytical methods are also used to accurately interpret and classify the meaning or context of a page's content and complement it with targeted ads. Semantic web content is closely linked to advertising to increase the viewer's interest in the advertised product or service.

Compatible sales

Combined marketing is a form of online advertising in which advertisers place campaigns with a large number of publishers, who are paid only for media payments where the advertiser receives web traffic. Web traffic is usually based on a call-to-action result or a measurable campaign result such as a web-based form or auction. Today, this is often accomplished by contracting with a related network.

Social Network Advertising

Social network advertising is a form of online advertising that is found on social networking sites such as Facebook. Advertising on social media can take the form of targeted ads purchased on social media, personalized advertising through internal ad networks, and ad serving on social networking apps through social networking advertising networks.

Search Engine Marketing (SEM)

Search engine marketing is a form of marketing that seeks to promote websites by increasing their visibility on search engine results pages (SERPs). SEM strategies include paid placement, content advertising, and paid placement, or free search engine optimization strategies to drive their ad placement. Advertisers pay every time users to click on their list and redirect to their website, rather than the ad itself. This program allows brands to improve search and gain information about their market.

Mobile Advertising

Mobile advertising is the ability of organizations and individuals to advertise their products or service through mobile devices. Mobile advertising is usually done through text messages or applications. The obvious advantage of mobile product advertising is that mobile devices such as smartphones are usually close to the owner throughout the day.

This provides an inexpensive way for brands to deliver targeted ads across all mobile platforms daily. Technologies such as location-based advertising give advertisers the ability to deliver ads closer to the actual buyer's location. Although ads come from a small mobile interface, mobile advertisers can deliver personalized messages to you, and thus be effective.

Various mobile marketing strategies include:

- Active screen advertising - Mobile phone owners enter into a third-party agreement that allows advertisers to play on their screen while their phone is idle to receive a discount or other promotion.
- App modification - Companies making apps, including games and videos, greatly improve their brand.
- DoubleClick for Advertisers - A Google service that allows companies to purchase specific keywords to increase their ad rankings in mobile search rankings.

Search Engine Optimization (SEO)

Search engine optimization (SEO) is the practice of using various strategies to allow websites to rank high in the Search Engine Optimization Pages (SERPs). Paid search engine advertising enhances website visibility and is accessible by displaying links to website landing pages at the top or bottom of the SERP. In contrast, SEO enhances website visibility and achievement by allowing the website to be positioned visually in search results when search engine users search for specific keywords and keywords.

Other SEO strategies include link building, onsite content optimization with targeted keywords, optimization of meta descriptions with targeted keywords, and optimization of blog content with targeted keywords. Many search engines work to find website users based on their search using complex algorithms that assess website authority, using a variety of techniques to measure the overall quality and usefulness of site content. SEO strategists aim to increase a site's reputation in the search engines by creating high-quality content using keywords that will be linked to other sites.

Local SEO is a trend that emerges in the realm of SEO. Local SEO involves creating content that is targeted to a particular site. It also includes the use of local listing sites to help establish a website presence in search results designed for local users.

Mobile Marketing

Mobile marketing is the practice of advertising brands on mobile devices such as smartphones, portable media players and tablets. This type of marketing allows advertisers and advertisers to promote products and services through mobile devices including mobile phones, smartphones, portable media players and tablets.

According to marketing professor Andreas Kaplan, mobile marketing, is "Any marketing activity done through a global network where consumers are constantly connected using a personal device". Because mobile marketing is done through wireless networks, it is also known as "wireless marketing". Marketing communications on mobile devices are usually done through text messages or applications. As consumers typically carry their mobile devices throughout the day, mobile marketing offers a less expensive way for products to deliver targeted messages to different forums.

QR Code Promotion: This is increasingly being used in mobile advertising campaigns to increase user engagement.

Types of Mobile Marketing

One of the most popular ways to advertise on a cell phone is to send text messages. In the early 2000s, the sale of cell phone messaging (SMS) services increased dramatically in Europe and parts of Asia. Therefore, SMS marketing has become an official advertising channel in both developed and developing economies around the world. On average, it is estimated that SMS messages are read within four minutes after being delivered to a cell phone. This makes mobile marketing more attractive to brands looking for high quality marketing communication channels that lead to conversions.

Unlike SMS, Multimedia Message Service (MMS) mobile marketing includes the delivery of images, text, audio and video. Almost all phones can send and receive regular MMS messages. Products can send and receive rich content via MMS A2P (app to person) mobile networks to mobile subscribers. On some networks, the brands are also able to support P2P (individual) messages.

App notifications are already popular for their use on smartphones running iOS and Android apps. These notifications appear at the top of the device screen and serve as an effective way to communicate directly with end users. While it may be considered a distraction for the end user, its long-term costs are lower than via SMS marketing.

Mobile game marketing offers additional opportunities for products that seek to deliver advertising messages within mobile games. Some companies sponsor all games to promote consumer engagement, a practice known as mobile advertising or ad-sponsored mobile games.

Mobile content marketing schemes provided by Yahoo! and Google allows brands to purchase keywords for mobile ads. Additionally, web forms on web pages can be used to integrate mobile text messaging resources to get reminders about meetings, seminars and other important events for users away from their laptop or desktop computers.

Quick Response (QR) codes also gained popularity after their first introduction in the European and Asian mobile markets. Serving as a visual interface for the page, QR codes allow users to jump to a custom mobile page. QR codes have been in use in North American mobile advertising since 2011.

Companies have seen technology as a very powerful tool for initiating customer engagement at a time when the marketing message is likely to arouse their deepest emotional reaction - a momentous moment - in the end user.

In addition to QR codes, other tools used by mobile advertisers to improve targeted messaging and reduce marketing costs include location-based services, Bluetooth technology, and nearby programs such as short message service - Cell Broadcasting (SMS-CB).

Advantages and Disadvantages of Mobile Marketing

Some of the important advantages of mobile phone marketing are the proximity of portable mobile devices, as well as the natural environment for using mobile phones, smartphones and tablets. Distributing customized promotional and promotional messages according to the recipient's location, location and personal interests via wireless networks makes mobile marketing less expensive considering the potential reach and wider audience.

However, mobile marketing processes present challenges regarding privacy concerns with user data. Push marketing tactics - mobile advertising delivered without the required consent of consumers - have resulted in a breach of privacy. Although mobile advertising has become increasingly popular with the growing use of tablets and smartphones, many concerns have arisen due to the human nature and proximity of mobile devices to users. Other major privacy concerns include mobile spam, personal identification, location information and wireless security.

Industry bodies including the Interactive Advertising Bureau and the Mobile Marketing Association have developed guidelines for blocking SPAM messages and the practice of network companies that sell member information to third parties.

However, these self-regulatory rules also apply to supporting advertisers who want to incorporate mobile marketing into their major marketing communications strategies.

Consumer Social Conduct

Understanding online and offline consumer behavior is essential to developing effective marketing communication strategies.

Communication Social Conduct

Digital and social media have encouraged brands to develop research strategies that focus on online consumer behavior. Observing and understanding how consumers behave and interact has led to the introduction of new semantic analysis technologies that allow companies to monitor consumer purchasing patterns based on shared and posted content. The data helps sales and marketing professionals improve segregation to guide prospects and customers.

Web User: The younger generations are using the web and mobile devices to increase their social media presence.

Consumer behavior

Traditionally, consumer behavior is the learning of individuals, groups, or organizations and processes that they use to select, purchase and dispose of products, services, entertainment, or ideas. Their purchase is intended to meet the needs. Studies have shown that consumer behavior is difficult to predict, even for marketing communications professionals. Relationship marketing, customer retention, customer relationship management (CRM) and personalization are all strategies used to assess customer behavior. However, consumer behavior is also influenced by internal factors such as census, psychographics (lifestyle), personality, motivation, knowledge, attitudes, beliefs, and emotions. Psychological factors include personal motivation, opinion, attitude and beliefs, while personal factors include income level, personality, age, occupation and lifestyle.

Types of Consumer Behavior

Extensive research is often used to understand what attracts consumers: colors, causes of thinking, images and sounds; all of these factors deal with psychological shopping behavior. Public procurement behavior includes identification and suggestion to inform certain consumer behavior. When a company hires a spokesman or personality to promote a product, it uses public procurement behavior to link the consumer's actions with that of the spokesperson or the personality involved. Similarly, psychographics is often used that provide insight into the lifestyle and personality traits of consumers.

Purchase status includes a specific situation or event that compels the consumer to purchase the product. Perhaps the fact that your peers buy the same product, or that a particular product has become "a symbol of." Whatever the reason, consumer behavior often plays a role.

Behavioral Trends Online

The advent of social media and social media platforms provides an easy way for people to connect on the web. People use social networking sites to meet new friends, find old friends, or find people with similar problems and interests. The information people post and share, as well as the relationships they build online, often transmit to the offline setting. While some critics have cited the decline in social media and social relationships as a result of the growth of social media, others point to the web and mobile technology as a way for younger generations to gain more social media.

Age and gender influence how the web and mobile devices are used and how decisions are made. While young women and older women are found to be more active in sending SMS messages, men send and receive additional audio calls. Psychologically, research shows that men seem to use technology faster and have more motivation to try new features. This may be due to differences in the attitudes of men and women toward new technologies. Women tend to view technology as a tool, while men tend to view it as fun.

Recognizing the link between social behavior and web technology is important for brands looking to advertise consumer-oriented products and services.

To implement an effective marketing communications strategy that integrates this data, companies use strategies such as behavioral identification to understand, collect and analyze consumer and offline consumer information.

Collecting and Analyzing Online Consumer Data

Products often use behavioral identification strategies to market to consumers based on their online behavior. The brands enhance the effectiveness of their campaigns by capturing data on web visitors who visit their website landing pages. Websites identify visitors by providing a unique ID cookie for each visitor to the site. This allows the forum to track users throughout their web journey and make legal decisions about what content to offer. However, if the conduct is done without the knowledge of the users, it may be regarded as a violation of browser security and illegal depending on national privacy, data protection and consumer protection laws. To monitor and evaluate behavior on social media sites, companies use analytics tools provided by social media platform or external vendors.

Also, this behavioral data can be combined with well-known demographic data and visitors' past purchasing history to generate a large number of data points that can be used to identify. Self-study behavior management systems on the site will monitor the visitor's response to site content and learn what might produce the desired conversion event (i.e. consumer purchase). Behavioral guidance can also be used to deliver multiple ads on many different sites based on the potential personalities of internet users. For example, a website might assume that an internet user is a male based on user visits to soccer sites with men.

Types of Consumer Digital Content Content

Consumer-generated content can be text, images, video or other digital information posted and shared by end users.

Types of Consumer Product Content

Twitter for iPad: Companies use consumer-generated content across all mobile applications such as tablet computers.

The type of digital content created, published and shared by web users varies depending on the media and communication technology available. The term "user-generated content" came into general use in 2005, following its rise in web publishing and new circles for the production of media content. Consumer content is used in areas that include problem-solving, news, gossip and research. The increase in consumer content, which has coincided with the rise of social media, reflects the increase in media production with new technologies that are accessible and affordable to the general public.

Consumer-generated content promotes collaboration and dialogue, as well as basic dialogue between individuals and organizations with similar interests, concerns or expertise. The web's ability to break the boundaries of space and time has opened the door to further opportunities for increased interaction and interaction between users and organizations that are physically different but digitally connected. This has generated a database of consumer information for companies that want to increase brand awareness and build customer relationships across all communication channels and communication channels.

Blogging, microblogging and social media are among the

most popular types of user-generated content. However, all digital media technologies are considered "user-generated content." Examples of these technologies include:

- Database answers to questions (e.g., Ask.com)
- Digital video (e.g., YouTube, Vimeo)
- Blogs (e.g., Blogger, Weebly)
- Microblogs (e.g., Tumblr, Twitter)
- Podcasting (e.g., iTunes)
- Update sites (e.g., Yelp, TripAdvisor)
- Social networking sites (e.g., Facebook, MySpace)
- Wikis (e.g., Wikipedia)

In addition to these digital media, user-generated content may also use a combination of open source, free software, and concessional licenses or related agreements to further reduce barriers to collaboration, capacity building and acquisition. Social networking sites like Facebook feature micro post features such as status updates, as well as "Like" and share buttons to promote interaction between users. Third-party websites and online publications help promote the publication and distribution of user-generated content by inserting separate bar widgets on their web pages. These digital icons allow users to interact directly with various social media accounts, where they can automatically post and share news stories, photos, videos and other content from a third-party website.

4 SOCIAL OBJECT

The Theory

Engeström described the concept of communication as a belief that all effective social interactions are focused on one thing - "the reason why people communicate alone and not something else." One way to describe a social object is a conversation between two or more people. People don't just talk - they often say "things around" them. For example, when I talk to my mom about flowers I sent her, flowers are something that affects the community.

Large numbers of digital chats revolve around social media, such as bookmarking, games, photos, stories, products, event, Facebook apps and more; these things become the subject of our conversations. Next, we may also be willing to share. I believe the good thing about digital communication is that it is very portable, and can be easily copied and redesigned across multiple channels and formats.

Do social media create communication on social media? You've probably heard the old saying that there are only six degrees of separation between just one person in the world and everyone (especially if your name is Kevin Bacon), so wouldn't it seem like sites, allowing people to communicate?

Can it be a great success too? This seems plausible at first, but the ability to connect and exchange information fails to explain what empowers these networks and creates such a difficult - and addictive - use for most people.

There have been many sites over the years that have allowed us to "connect" easily. SixDegrees.com, a popular site since the dotcom era, has done just that, yet it is no longer available. LinkedIn is a great site, connecting a lot of people, but it has never exploded in the same way as Facebook, despite its long presence. These sites connect people without helping them create social media that gives them a domain where they can connect.

A good example of a social media site? Flickr. Creative social elements are not just images, but collections of images, URLs and even comments. Flickr expands and expands - quantum jumps from the realm of private images, reserved for viewing only by people who know the uploader. Any image on Flickr is relevant and accessible - and shared by unrelated people. Twitter spreads a variety of social media, too. An item is usually a URL, but users are usually object as usernames can be shared. Comments themselves can be objects, people repeating themselves, and where new conversations are created.

The question of what makes social media even more interesting is when we look at prosperous community-based environments and find that people who do not have close social relationships are somehow connected. More interestingly, these connections often exceed one network, in the blogosphere. Some conversations go beyond a small circle of close-knit ones, moving between different sites and occasionally attracting large crowds, producing a great deal of influence. That is a far cry from the social networking site "friend."

Could there be a fundamental force behind this? Social object theory says that things are less powerful. It explains why social networking sites are more likely to be successful than non-successful ones, and it explains why people who do not have normal social relationships find reasons to connect.

Applying social media theory to marketing campaigns

Social media theory has an impact on advertising, and at Razorfish ™, we have been quietly using it for the past 18 months, with very good results.

Ready to hear what we have learned?

At first, some people in our group thought the theory simply meant the obvious; we were not sure how to use it in digital campaigns but we thought it was an important opportunity. We had to start reading, and, as there was little written about public affairs, we were on our way to the discovery. First, we began to consider the theory during the creative phase of the project. We soon found out that by changing our mindset to answer the question, "what makes a good community thing?" We can rethink our ideas or improve existing ones.

In the early months, we did not always have the desire to produce public goods, but as time went on, our projects took on natural features that one could associate with objects; the objects themselves took over the structures caused by the bacteria, thus becoming socially viable. Now that a lot of projects, which consider public object theory, have passed our doors, we are using it more strategically.

It has also been the basis of major campaigns, especially our efforts of the Smirnoff Secret Party of Diageo which formed a new foundation as a social media campaign by not including one thing but many to allow for greater vision, especially through social media rather than just a product website. In this example, the main social media feature was "The Smirnoff Secret Party" which allowed users on social media to discuss the event, and who the mysterious DJs could be and where the event could be held. Small community items have been used in a way that is confusing and confusing in the pursuit of digital values for free tickets.

Explicit clues [objects] inspired to occur on social media platforms between users.

The GPS, embedded in the indexed blog, allows users to enter the real world to find hidden tickets that, for example, may be recorded under a park bench. These real-world tickets often provoke debate and debate.

About Lipton Tea (Unilever), we created a site full of small game-based items to allow for something bigger - brain training. This was in contact with an Amino acid called L-Theanine, which has recently been shown to keep tea drinkers relaxed and alert compared to other beverages.

As the digital environment changes and social changes, I believe that using some of the findings and processes below will continue to help us produce better campaigns. We still need to learn more about social media and its role in the lives of our consumers, but as we move from outdated monologue marketing models to chat-driven advertising, this idea can help us find better ways to truly engage with our customers.

Here is what we have learned so far from the theory:

- Social media can take many forms, including links, videos, photos, bookmarks, widgets, events and products such as the iPhone. He may also be abstract (e.g. Christianity or Postmodernism). The more compact the object, the greater the likelihood that it will succeed.
- Public items do not need to be infected. It may be enough simply to make them "available". For example, with current or relevant news items (e.g. a plane crashing into the Hudson River) it may be necessary to make sure that your social media item (perhaps an article or video related to chat) is ready for search, so users can find it.
- Public renegotiations in traditional campaigns can be extremely difficult. For example, a PUSH message like "Taste Like Summer in a Bottle" tells the consumer what to think, which poses a

daunting challenge for agencies to build digital communications. In contrast, Burger King's Whopper Sacrifice campaign asks users to give up 10 friends on Facebook exchange with a free Whopper. This great idea in itself was a public one, not just a conversation but also running support features such as the application on Facebook.

To make the campaign more community-based, we recommend the following practices:

- Describe your communication resources well in advance; they may even form the basis of a larger view.
- Decide whether your campaign is done with one thing - or perhaps thousands of them. For example, is your promotional video a reality, or do you provide consumers with more creative tools in addition to the theme you have provided?
- Find out what makes your social object or objects social and make your social item valuable, relevant and real to consumers.
- Make sure your items are portable, free of charge and do not copy. Ask yourself if your social media item can skip mediums. For example, can your video be easily explained by a blogger or a tweeter?
- Find out how long your item will last. Does it contain stories or articles? Allow online debate, discussion and interaction around your stuff. Consider creating objects that are intentionally tagged, tracked, and rated.
- Do not assume that the object you are communicating with, automatically, brands or products of your website. However, your projects probably already have social media

features. Identify, build and prepare.

Another quote from Hugh McLeod of gapingvoid.com, summarizes how we as agencies and brands need to think as we embrace social ideologies: "The most important word on the internet is not 'search.' The most important word on the Internet is 'Share.'"

What is Social Object

The business world is rapidly evolving into the digital age. With the internet, you have been able to find products and services for a variety of needs. Similarly, transactional transactions can be made between the seller and the buyer without face-to-face contact. The whole process can be done online, from ordering to courier delivering your ordered goods. In the future, we may not have to leave our homes to care for our daily needs. In that digital marketing needs to be used in sales today.

This situation is a challenge for retailers to follow digital trends, if they do not want to lag and cannot compete in the market. For both retailers working in the offline industry and already entering the online marketplace, learning, and using digital marketing for their business is a must.

In the digital market, there is a high value of social media that is often overlooked by online advertisers. Although this number is very important to note. The following definition relates to the importance of social media in digital marketing.

Every good marketing campaign needs a public object. It is the very thing that unites people. It may give people the same purpose or simply give them something to talk about. It promotes and enhances human coexistence. And with a marketing campaign, is key, as it paves the way for virality and community growth. (Traders want word-for-word transmission!) The most obvious example of a social media item would be a baseball: The boy and his father get a good quality bond time playing catch in front of the yard. Football becomes a social phenomenon that allows them to do this.

In the marketing world, a good example of a public object would be the gallery of the Kraft Oreo Cookie Moments Gallery. The basis is clear: To help celebrate their 100th anniversary, Oreo has asked his fans to share with them their favorite Oreo photos, videos and stories and they will "share them with the world". Oreo fans would upload their own "Oreo Moment" via Facebook or their small campaign base. These moments were then displayed on Facebook and microsite, and they were able to fully share on each follower's social graph via Facebook. Every minute of Oreo became a public object. Can the Oreo Cookie itself also be a public good? Certainly. Many brands themselves are major social product brands. In fact, the guy who represented the term "public object" says that unless your product is a public item, you probably do not sell it. Any Apple product (iPhone, iPad, etc.) is a good example of something social.

To a large extent, effective social networks should define their concept of a social object. For example, Flickr uses user-generated images as public objects. Fun or Digg uses URLs. Facebook uses images, URLs, and status updates. But what about LinkedIn? A convincing argument as to why some social media platforms work and others do not argue that effective, sustainable social networks should focus on "object-oriented".

The community as part of the social environment both in the family, in the rental companies, and the residential areas, must have certain relationships and relationships. This happens from sticking to each other for the same needs or reasons. From this, social factors are understood as the reasons why a person can be in a particular community, and then make and live in a group.

Likewise in the online business industry, social media is needed in digital advertising to be used in them. A common problem is when an online business aims to make a profit and not focus on customers. For public goods to be released, this amount when used will have a significant impact on sales.

You need to use social media if you want to get good results in digital marketing. Like increasing the number of followers on social media, the impact of promoters, the impact of the buzzer, and more. Social media is a gem that makes your audience want to establish a relationship with your business. What makes your customers want to know your brand and brand?

Besides using social media in digital marketing, you can make fatal mistakes in a promotion. For example, you offer a promo on the condition that your potential customers should follow your Instagram account. You may think that many customers will be interested in the promotions offered, but ignoring this type of approach can burden your customers, even before they buy your product. The psychological burden can damage the reputation of your product if it turns out that your offer does not meet the expectations of consumers. The worst effect will either give you negative feedback or stop tracking your account. Therefore, public resources are needed.

In the world of digital marketing, careful and creative scrutiny is needed to create social media between products and consumers. This method can be used to create content marketing, especially on social media, which allows you to create great social media content. To create such content, you must include meaningful, new, and progressive features. In its definition, rational means the needs of your customers and compliance with the products offered. New targeted content must be new or never created by competitors. In addition, sustainability means that content is used by the audience for a longer period of time.

That is a discussion of the important role of social media in digital marketing that is important for you to understand. With the right social tool, you can increase the number of customers and sales. And do not forget to advertise with the Froggy Ads service, you can start by advertising your product, so that later you increase the number of visitors to your online business website. Froggy Ads is an online advertising service that can help you manage all your product campaigns. helps you direct the targeted advertising you want and gives you many marketing options for your product.

Something like the collaboration itself could be a kind of social thing. Consider the so-called social business model. In this view, the company, from the product, customer service, engineering, marketing, and so on, all connected not only with each other but with their external customers. Edelman Digital's Michael Brito has an informative infographic of what a social business model looks like. Managers of public enterprises must acquire their public assets if they want to see their clients and employees work together, and discuss and transform their ideas into tangible results. Dell's IdeaStorm is encouraging in this regard.

As a social media marketer or an online community manager, you should often disclose your social media content. How do you do this? There is no tried and true model here. My advice is to start by working as a team facilitator. Listen, listen, listen. Chart topics that are often discussed or products, feelings, problems, constructive feedback, etc. You will then have a short list of themes for which you can work. Get community members involved not only in what the community's goal is, but what the process and rewards (if any) can be. This can be important for sharing. Remember that in the end, you will not be in control of the thing itself. However, you can help with the process and the result.

Not All Shared are Equal

And at the same time the fact is that social media is a great opportunity for furniture retailers. Social media has become a major source of information (or other facts, if you prefer) to many consumers and the furniture buying cycle is naturally committed to sharing ideas and discussing furniture items on social media. This practice has been confirmed by numerous studies that have shown, for example, that platforms like Pinterest are already used by more than 30% of consumers to get decorative ideas and that social media discussions play an important role in consumer decisions to do.

However, based on our awareness of how consumers share interior design ideas on social media, all sharing is unequal. While 'traditional' sharing of images, e.g. liking and voting for merchant images of various living room sets, creates high traffic volume and builds fan communities, conversations tend to be short-lived and do not build real product relationships (no wonder that as your customer may follow competitors). On the other hand, when consumers share relevant information, for example, product design photos and combinations they have made with your products, discussions often take place in small communities but are personally involved and often last longer. Excellent results, we believe, are achieved by combining these two strategies and closing the dialogue between a focused product and personalized sharing. Examples of this are competitions that allow customers to link your products to their homes (Fagmoebler, DHY.com) and 'themed rooms' (e.g. La-Z-Boy) not only provide decorative ideas but also allow customers to translate ideas into their home environment and tailor them to suit their will. And when customers have personal contact with your products, they often continue conversations within their social network (after all, now it's about their home decoration) and later back to your product, for example, if someone else. on their social network selects new furniture.

Collaboration as a Community Object

Every conversation and marketing campaign needs something social, something that brings people together and gives them something to talk about. Sharing photos of decorating ideas within a social network often serves as a great starting point for conversation but, unless someone is a person who loves interior decoration, the bad truth is that 'favorites' are cheaper. Conversations usually end after one or two comments. And this is the reason why we focus on building partnerships and sharing features. When customers can share real interior designs, not just their photos, their friends can take part in the design process itself, that is, suggest and visualize a different selection of materials, other product items, or completely new interior designs, and get more involved. This not only deepens and deepens the dialogue surrounding your product but also exposes the customer communication network more to your products. And we believe that, even though only a small percentage of consumers may regularly engage in 'internal social design', these consumers are often the leaders of ideas on their social networks and that is why they are the long-term promoters of your product.

Moving on to Public Business Models

Focusing on social cohesion instead of just social sharing brings businesses another important benefit. Promoting direct communication between customers and business employees it does more than just create product awareness. It allows the business to engage in ongoing customer conversation, provide real-time expert advice, and assist customers in their purchase choices, that is, to replicate the different channels that good sellers always do in the store. In areas where the sales cycle already involves many parties, such as high-end furniture, commercial furniture and home development, the social business model can be easily expanded to include third-party service providers, such as interior designers, consultants, architects and builders. By allowing these service providers and customers to come together and collaborate on your shared platform you can become the center of a broader ecosystem, create more exposure for your product and, at the end of the day, sell more.

5 ESSENTIAL SKILLS IN SOCIAL MARKETING

A social marketer manager can be a salesperson, strategist, copyist, designer, analyst, and customer service representative sometimes all in one day. As a person who loves challenges, that diversity is one of the things that drew me to community service.

Managing all these various responsibilities requires communication managers to develop several important marketing skills and communication skills. An effective communication platform expert brings both solid and soft skills to the table, both types that take time and effort to improve. Strong skills such as data analysis and copying can be easily learned and trained, while soft skills like editing and communication can be very difficult to learn, but very important.

One of the most rewarding and challenging aspects of social work is that you have not yet completed your studies. You just have to be more discriminating with the help you render toward other people. The more you focus on developing these skills, the more you will be able to drive results, get real business impact and improve your skills as a social worker.

Develop your social media skills with the right social media tools

Now that you have mastered the skills of this article, start using social media management tools to further your social success.

1. Communication

At its core, social media is a platform for communication — so as a communications expert, it is important to have strong communication skills that are flexible to fit any platform, media, number of characters, or audience. For example, one day you can often switch between contacting clients in the mailbox, meeting with your product team to share feedback, writing briefly to start a creative project, or compiling a public listening analysis to share with leaders. You should be able to convey ideas to many participants.

➢ Communicating with people

As your brand's voice to customers in the community, you should be able to stop what you are doing right away to jump to a trending topic or handle an unhappy customer complaint. And you are not just talking about writing; you use emojis, videos, GIFs, photos, stickers and anything else you have to convey your message clearly and attractively.

➢ Communication with your manager and team

Internally, you should also be able to communicate effectively with your supervisor, peers and participants across all teams. You must talk to any internal participant about your social media strategy, content distribution system and the impact of your work. The ability to explain how your communications career moves a business forward is one of the most important skills any communications professional can develop.

Finally, strong communication skills are key to

improving in-house education and training. While your social media team may earn money for your company's social media marketing efforts, you can also work to train people from departments such as customer support, marketing and creative to support and use social media in their fields.

Resources for building your communication skills

TED Talks on communication: Hear from some of the world's most inspiring speakers on enhancing your conversations, digital communication and storytelling skills.

Spirit Insights: blogs talking about increasing the influence and impact of business on society.

2. Writing

While many skills can help convey your message to the community, the core of communication always returns to the written word.

Leading media executives are excellent copywriters and brilliant digital speakers who not only integrate but also enhance, the voice of their product in communication. From a compelling copy of the ad to a clever design, you should know how to write a short, provocative copy for your audience. The Il Makiage cosmetics brand did a great job of this, pairing the green captions with their colorful, full-length art to tell a story and connect with their audience with pop culture experience.

Successful writers are also able to organize their writing for different audiences and forums. For example, while you can use up to 2,200 characters in your Instagram captions, data has shown that the most attractive length of Instagram captions is between 138-150 characters.

While writing is an important skill for the social media platform to create engaging content and discussions, it is also important for your work. If you are asked to contribute to your company's blog, give management an understanding of your strategy or make a case for growing your social media budget, there will probably be some writing involved. The ability to express yourself through clear, well-thought-out emails, strategies and presentations will help your ideas to be impressive.

Resources for improving your writing

Hemingway Editor: This website and app can help make your writing more accessible and readable. While this is mainly intended for long form writing, it can also be used to create an effective communication post.

Grammar Girl: You can double check the thorny grammar questions by Googling "grammar girl" and any of your questions.

Merriam-Webster's Twitter feed: Grow your vocabulary with the words of the day, learn the differences between similar words and enjoy a little reading when this dictionary writes Tweets about words that have been misused or built into the news cycle.

3. Creation

Diversity is one of the biggest product challenges in the full space of the social media platform. Every social media manager wants to create interesting, relevant and buzz-filled content, but it takes ingenuity to come up with brilliant ideas.

When it comes to social media skills, art is highly flexible. Creating helps social media managers:

- Develop risky social campaigns
- Create attractive, multimedia content
- Consider all the aesthetic details of a public post, from photos to links to copy formatting
- Lead productive ideas that reflect the positive ideas of their team partners
- Respect and amplify their product voice and status
- Along with being creative, have a sense of

humor and the ability to improve in any situation.

Resources for translating your creativity

Creative Mornings Events: Creative Mornings is a series of morning art community events. Join a local event or online community to connect with other curious, creative, design and community leaders.

Improvement classes: Taking better classes can teach you how to solve problems differently and give you more confidence in managing customer responses faster.

Fast Company and Campaign: These two books offer thought-provoking and critical comments on the world of creative advertising. Read on to find out more about creating products and strategies, industry-leading campaigns and thought leadership.

Online Classes: LinkedIn Learning and Skillshare, along with a host of other resources, offer online classes on everything from writing to mobile photography. Canva has basic non-design classes that you can download online to improve your graphic design skills.

4. High efficiency and quality planning

You can't manage a social media strategy without managing your time wisely, doing well and planning the two communication skills needed.

As a social media platform, you should not only think about campaigns and distribution strategies, but you should lead and implement these programs from start to finish. To do this on a scale, a competent social worker will use the tools, policies and procedures of their social presence to keep all moving pieces straight. Using a social media calendar is one of the best ways to keep content organized and organized.

Resources to improve efficiency and order

Pomodoro Technique and boxing time: You can worry

about a good copy all day ... but sometimes you have 50 messages to write and plan to stand between you and your weekend. Setting aside a specific time to work on a specific task helps me to keep things in perspective.

Value-setting: Sometimes everything about communicating sounds urgent — but you have to start with the most important things.

5. Traditional and digital marketing

If you see your role as focused on achieving community goals, I want to challenge you to think more deeply. Social sits at the crossroads of marketing, customer information and marketing and is the source of such valuable business intelligence.

Yet despite the diverse social environment, 47% of social media advertisers say that developing community strategies that underpin overall business principles is their first challenge. Your ability to integrate your social strategy into larger advertising and business objectives is what will take your career to the next level.

To create a socially influential business strategy, it is important to build an understanding of other traditional and digital marketing methods: email, events, the leading generation, PR and more. This information will help you put the community within the context of how your product interacts with its customers, conducts sales and ultimately generates revenue.

Resources to increase your marketing ability

Marketing promoters: Leaders like Joe Pulizzi and Seth Godin have withstood the test of time with the wisdom of marketing all social media professionals can use.

Textbooks and marketing courses: I find myself referring to my old social science textbooks and marketing research all the time! If you study at work, check out LinkedIn Learning Lessons for marketing and strategies.

Books by Malcolm Gladwell: Read "The Tipping Point"

or "Outliers" to strengthen your understanding of human behavior and marketing.

6. Customer care

Customer care is a communication platform skill that combines customer service, human skills and an eye for opportunities. Developing a community customer care strategy is an important part of being a communications manager.

According to the latest Sprout Social Index ™, 33% of consumers prefer to access brands on social media for a customer service question or question. Not only must you listen to and understand the concerns, demands and recommendations of current customers, but you should also be involved in what your future customers can say. It is equally important to be able to read the DM and see the "why" after which the customer is upset, as it is to be able to find a clever way to surprise and delight a long-time fan.

For example, women's clothing and ban.do brands always entertain their customers? When one of their recurring customers shared a product proposal on Twitter, ban.do respond immediately to let their customer know that their response had been heard and shared with the team.

As a social media manager, you are a great champion of your product. Understanding customer care enables you to make a positive impact on the hearts and minds of your community. Making your interactions personal by referring to chat history can help take daily engagements and make you a special moment.

Services to improve the care of your customers

Zendesk's Relate Blog and Events: Check out Relate for the best consistent content on relationships, customer service and leadership.

Podcasts: Customer care begins with customer awareness.

7. Making connections

One of the most important aspects of social media is human nature. This means that establishing and building digital relationships is still an integral part of any communication platform manager.

Our research found that 64% of consumers want products to contact them on social media. If they feel connected to a product, 57% of people will increase their spending on that product and 76% will prefer that product over a competitor. There are always new communications to be made in communication, and leading social media professionals are active and creative when it comes to building.

That being said, everyone has a different level of comfort and skill when it comes to connecting and sharing. As a social media manager, feel free to try, improve your brand voice and understand the state of how you play or risk yourself. What has worked for Wendy's on the #NuggsForCarter exchange will not apply to all brands, and that's fine.

As valuable as 1: 1 communication, this daily communication also provides the answer to one of the biggest challenges for social media marketers. It have been found that the top challenge for social workers is to identify and understand their target audience.

As a social media platform, the details of your audience size and unique contact information for your fans give you an important insight into what your audience wants and needs.

Understanding and communication services for your audience

CMX Facebook Group, Summit & resources: CMX is an organization of community experts to connect, grow and prosper. Check out their free resources and annual conference.

Sprout Social Index: annual report on social status

contains data and details of what consumers want from the community and what marketers are doing.

Data report: What consumers want from brands in a different community: In this consumer trends report, we conducted a consumer survey to understand their desire for greater communication — with their favorite products and each other — and how today's brands benefit when social networking.

8. Intelligence

As we all know, social conditions are moving fast and even the most well-laid plans can quickly become useless.

The ability to move around quickly and respond to a new trend, opportunity or problem is an important skill of the social media platform. On a day-to-day basis, speed and flexibility can help you respond more strongly to a frustrated customer (or more appreciative fan) in more sensitive and personalized ways.

It is also important to be quick when talking about your long-term strategy. Community strategies should be as powerful and flexible as the platforms on which they rely. As a communications manager, it is important that you try different strategies, or re-evaluate your strategy completely, to adapt to new trends, implement business changes or back down from lower results.

Reading your data, listening to feedback (customer and internal) and maintaining a sense of social inclination can all make a social marketer manager much faster.

Resources

Know Your Meme: This website can help keep up with the daily development of new memes.

Twitter Trends sidebar is a useful tool for keeping an eye out for emerging styles and new content.

Google Alerts: Install keyword alerts for a variety of reasons: stay informed about online companies, industry news and world news.

9. Data analysis

We're all familiar with end-of-month reporting, but skilled social media executives look at data and make it more effective than starting in the month.

➤ Understanding both quantity and quality data

Those of us who have worked in communications for a while may be aware of quality-back information in the western part of social life, you needed to be able to present accurate, abundant data to give your total effort to that quality data. it was often pushed aside.

Today, with the growing importance of public listening, it is important to develop both data analytics skills and quality to understand the full picture and social functioning.

➤ Communicate your ideas to participants

Social performance reporting is a good first step, but analysis means looking at your data and being able to identify trends, develop recommendations and interact with the app. The analysis gives you something solid and important that you can bring to your manager, your partners and other departments.

Resources for building your analytical skills

#SproutChat with Joe Wadlington of Twitter: Watch the conversation with Joe to learn more about using both quantity and quality data.

Updated

If you have already mastered all of these nine social media skills, congratulations — you still have work to do. Socializing is a lifelong learning process, and continuing to hone these skills will benefit you at all stages of your career.

I see skills development as a way to buy out time for other things. For example, if you are already very organized and efficient, you can spend a lot of time developing one of your weak skills, building your product through verbal interviews or preparing to enter human management.

Additionally, doing well in one place may open the door for your next visit — for example, if you are a good data analyst, you can probably become a great spy expert! Or if connecting is your job, you may be an incredible community manager.

CONCLUSION: TIPS FOR SUCCESSFUL SOCIAL MARKETING

1. Know your audience
The first step in building a successful social media marketing strategy is to know who your target audience is or to determine who your product is intended for. How do you determine which product your brand will appeal to?

That's what your industry is up to.

Before you get into the kind of people you should target, you need to clearly understand why your product or service exists, and who it works for. What problems does it solve? The answer to this question will help you to move on to points # 2 and # 3: determine the number of people in your audience and the type of audience.

> Demographics (age, gender, location, etc.)

Your product will fit well with certain segments of people, and you may not be very compatible with other segments. For example, if you are an e-commerce store selling cosmetics, you may want to focus on your efforts to reach women, say between the ages of 16 and 50, and use forums similar to these figures, such as Facebook or Instagram.

> Type of audience

Once you know what your industry is dealing with, this step should be relatively simple. You need to find out which type of audience will benefit most from your product. Bloggers, Professional Professionals, Individual Buyers? Or, if you look at the larger scale and then SMBs, Businesses, and Products?

Once you've minimized that, the next step is to decide which community channels to focus on.

2. Decide which social networks work best with your social media marketing strategy

There will be 4.4 billion social media users in the coming years, and that number will only grow. Sites like Facebook, Instagram, and Pinterest are all very important platforms when it comes to spreading brand awareness or engaging with your customers. The question remains, however: which forums should you be advertising?

It may seem like working on all of them is a good idea, as this will increase your reach and help spread the word, but that is not the best strategy. Being on all social media platforms will make it difficult for you to manage them all effectively and you will find yourself in the position of "Jack of all trades, master of none". One of the most effective strategies is to select a few community channels for your marketing strategy that will work best for your Target Audience audience and focus your efforts on advertising your product there.

3. Present and expand your profiles

Setting up your site is a good step, but introducing your sites and forums alone will not be enough to get you started on your strategy. To fully realize the power of your marketing strategies and to effectively drive traffic to your site, you should use processes to improve your community strategies.

Whether you're focusing too much on Pinterest

advertising or over-emphasizing Facebook strategies, it's important to make sure your profiles are directed in their direction. Your services and marketing should be built to continuously improve traffic using promotional strategies, such as improving visual content, using blog posts, and even using videos to reach your audience.

The word "doing well" can make people feel frustrated, but the process of developing your social networks is not as difficult as it may sound and may be beyond your control. To improve your profiles once you've submitted them, spend some time exploring the people you want to reach, and how you can better reach those people. Social media posts can be redirected and enhanced using the appropriate hashtags, making sure the images are neatly organized using a different text, and including common keywords in your posts. Whether you use videos on YouTube as a source of marketing, or your Facebook post is your bread and butter, profile improvement is important.

4. Create important content for your social media strategy

Now that you have decided who you should target and where you should advertise your product, you can begin working on creating the content of your social media marketing strategy. This is one of the strongest tips on social media because content is a form of social media marketing for all platforms, including Facebook, Instagram, Pinterest, and more.

The type of content you create depends on the public accounts you are sending to. Posts work differently for different public profiles, so it makes sense to edit the content relevant to each public profile. For example, posting quotes on Instagram is a great way to get involved, but doing the same on Facebook may not guarantee the same access. Posting links to Facebook is quick and easy, but connecting to Instagram requires extra steps for both the poster and the buyer – even though they both use the news effectively to communicate.

There are several tools you can use to create high quality content types easily. For example, Viraltag uses Canva to create attractive and attractive posts.

5. Automatically post to your social media channels

In theory, posting content on social media seems simple enough: design posts, and upload them online every few hours to engage your customers. But how do you know when to post? And if you have to keep posting all day, how do you do that without logging in and out of each public profile and uploading by posting? Perhaps most importantly: How do you reduce the time spent on social media goals, but make sure you still drive traffic to your website? These are some of the most important questions you can ask as you go about searching for editing tools.

The answer? A social media marketing tool. Tools like Viraltag, Buffer, Hootsuite, or AgoraPulse make it easy to select, manage, and edit the content on a single dashboard, which effectively saves 5-6 hours each week without losing readers, missing missions, or losing money!

These sites are typically designed to host multiple platforms, including regular ones like Facebook, and even to include rare (but less commonly used) sites like Pinterest, and they are often trusted tools for communication professionals.

You can edit the content weeks in advance, and the tool will automatically post those posts to social media within a specified time. All you have to do is make sure you have enough posts and enough articles listed in your content line to complete those weeks.

You can also use your old posts to make sure you don't run out of topics to discuss. Redesigning the purpose of your old content is a great way to make sure all your visitors — old and new — see your post. This way, you get miles above your best-performing posts and increase traffic to your website, while your content is more accessible. It is also important to remember, considering all of these marketing tips on social media, that frequent posting on different social profiles requires different strategies. For example, you can post more pins on Pinterest per day than you can post on Facebook. Determine the most important sites, budget your time, and create original content in advance to increase click-through and stick to your content strategy, all without sacrificing organization and time.

6. Increase your compliance with contests and sweepstakes

Everyone loves competition, as most people are thrilled to get something for free – even if that item comes from a business they did not know before. Offering your products or services — or offering something you like from another product or service — is a great way to enhance your engagement, grow your loyal followers, and direct your target audience.

To use this tool effectively, you should encourage people who see your post to share it, too. Whether you use Facebook, Instagram, or another site that makes sharing easy and convenient, make sharing your given posts an integral part of your competition or sweepstakes. This ensures that you reach the total number of followers in your offering.

Before you create your own dedicated posts on social media, try to decide what will be most important to your followers and how much you can offer something. If you are not yet established as a product, your fans may not be interested in competing or sweepstakes incorporating your products or services and making more than one gift per month can be very immersed in your income.

To make a gift successfully, you can put your products or services next to another product or service to increase the interest people can have in your offering, and get your brand, products, or services there, regardless of what it means to make a gift individually. per month, or once a quarter.

7. Connect with influencers in your niche

Communicating and interacting with influential people in your niche is probably one of the most effective ways to make your organization's posts more recognizable and spread brand awareness. If you have a promoter in your team, approving or commenting on your product/service, the name will spread, and it will spread quickly!

This is because promoters are already building strong relationships with their followers. When they talk about a product in their video content, their audience knows that the product is worth a try, because they trust the promoter's judgment. If you have this confidence on your side, hit gold.

To ensure that your product is seen by the promoter and stands out from the crowd, you need to establish long-term relationships with the team you have built. This is how social media platforms like Facebook can turn photos and news into favorites, clicks, and visitors to increase your sales and loyal followers.

Here's a 4-step guide on how to connect with the person promoting your product (by emphasizing how to connect on social media):

i) Identify influencers in your niche

Step # 1 is finding out who influences your industry. You can use tools like Buzzsumo and NinjaOutreach to search for a keyword and determine who your main promoters are, what their current fan lists are and what they follow and what trends they represent.

ii) Connect with them on social media

LinkedIn: When marketing a B2B product, LinkedIn is an important platform for you to engage with your promoters to build a strong marketing team. Send promoters to choose a connection request, and a personal message about how you know them, and what you like about their work. Follow their LinkedIn page, and share their posts, too. Working with people requires that you give as much as you can.

Facebook: Connect with influencers on Facebook. Using Facebook is a smart way to get in front of your target audience, and reach both the B2B and the B2C community. Search for a promoter's Facebook page, follow it, and comment / like their posts and photos. It's also a good idea to share their Facebook photos, and tag them, as it's a great opportunity for recognition.

Twitter: Twitter is probably the best social media platform for direct contact with promoters. Follow their Twitter handle, write the content they post (including photos), and make sure you mention it when you share their content, so they can get notified and recognized.

Instagram: It doesn't mean that to get the promoter's attention, you have to follow their feed, and like and comment on their posts. Redirecting their posts through apps like Repost is a great way to make them aware of your efforts.

iii) Enter Your Influences

After you follow and connect with them on social media, from Facebook to LinkedIn (and don't forget blogs and Pinterest!), send them a personal email. Here are three examples of well-executed influencer outreach lessons!

iv) Maintain your communication relationships

Make sure you still work with the promoters you hope to work with on social media, to maintain your relationship. You do not want to be frustrated if you cannot get the right pitch so invest in a good capo.

A solid social media marketing strategy does not involve rocket science, but it does require planning, research, and, above all, discipline to stick to the system until you see results. If you should not see the results you want, go back and do this job again, to see where you might have misplaced thinking about your marketing strategies on your business forums!

8. Measure, analyze and expand

Once you have established a rhythm, set aside a timeline to measure, analyze, and improve your marketing and communication strategies. These three steps are essential to successfully manage your community strategies, as they ensure that you evaluate all your ongoing marketing efforts, evaluate their effectiveness, and eliminate or modify strategies that do not successfully market your business or increase your reach. Whether you focus on Facebook, YouTube videos, or especially working with LinkedIn, you should constantly evaluate your business objectives and the strategies you use to achieve your goals.

Balancing your social media accounts can be difficult, and it requires checking your business with a good dental comb — a process that may require you to set aside your identity. After all, not all the strategies you create will work, and you have to be willing to sacrifice to make your sales goals, increase your traffic, and produce content that affects communities and always gets results.

FAQ Social Media Marketing Tips

How can I improve my social media marketing?

Here are some tips on how to improve your social media marketing:

1. Find out who your target audience is and who your products are.
2. Choose the best social media channel that best suits your social media marketing strategy.
3. Configure your social media accounts.
4. Create important communication content.
5. A network that influences within your niche.

What are the 3 marketing strategies of the social media platform?

The 3 best marketing strategies on social media are:
1. Find your goals and work out a plan that is consistent with your goals.
2. Understand your audience well.
3. Make it a practice to do research.

What are the five most effective marketing strategies on social media?

The five most effective marketing strategies for social media are:
1. Always teach and give your audience value.
2. Create a variety of content.
3. Increase customer loyalty, reviews, and user-generated content.
4. Focus on the best social media platform that works for your strategy.
5. Connect with other influencers in your niche.

How do beginners use social media marketing?

Here are the steps for beginners to navigate and use social media marketing:
1. Set wise and targeted goals for your strategy
2. Set KPIs
3. Describe your appropriate audience
4. Pay close attention to your competitors
5. Plan your communication strategy.

THANKS

Dear reader, I hope you enjoyed this book and want to let me know your thought.

You can also use the following link:
https://www.amazon.com/review/create-review/

REFERENCES

Bajarin, B. 2011. "Could What Happened to MySpace Happen to Facebook?", Time Online, viewed 20 September 2011, http://techland.time.com/2011/07/15/could-what-happened-to-myspace-happen-to-facebook/

Bampo, Mauro, Michael T. Ewing, Dineli R. Mather, David Stewart, and Mark Wallace. 2008. "The Effects of the Social Structure of Digital Networks on Viral Marketing Performance." Information Systems Research 19: 273-290.

Bourlakis, Michael, Savvas Papagiannidis, and Feng Li. 2009. "Retail Spatial Evolution: paving the way from traditional to metaverse retailing." Electronic Consumer Research 9:135-148.

Breuer, A. 2011, Democracy promotion in the age of social media: risks and opportunities, Briefing Paper, Department 'Governance, Statehood, Security', German Development Institute.

Campbell, Colin, Leyland F. Pitt, Michael Parent, and Pierre R. Berthon. 2011. "Understanding Consumer Conversations around Ads in a Web 2.0 World." Journal of Advertising 40:87-102.

Casaló, Luis V., Flavián Carlos, and Miguel Guinalíu. 2008. "Promoting Consumer's Participation in Virtual Brand

Communities: A New Paradigm in Branding Strategy." Journal of Marketing Communications 14: 19-36.

Castells, M. 2009, Communication Power, Oxford University Press, Oxford.

Cha, Jiyoung. 2009. "Shopping on Social Networking Websites: Attitudes towards real versus virtual items." Journal of Interactive Advertising, 10: 77-93.

Cheong, Hyuk Jun, and Margaret A. Morrison. 2008. "Consumers' Reliance on Product Information and Recommendations Found in UGC." Journal of Interactive Advertising 8: 38-49.

Chi, Hsu-Hsien. 2011. "Interactive Digital Advertising VS. Virtual Brand Community: Exploratory Study of User Motivation and Social Media Marketing Responses in Taiwan." Journal of Interactive Advertising 12: 44-61.

Chu, Shu-Chuan. 2011. "Viral advertising in social media: Participation in Facebook groups and responses among college-aged users." Journal of Interactive Advertising 12: 30-43.

Cox, Shirley A. 2010. "Online Social Network Member Attitude Toward Online Advertising Formats." MA thesis, The Rochester Institute of Technology.

Curran, Kevin, Sarah Graham, and Christopher Temple. 2011. "Advertising on Facebook." International Journal of E-Business Development 1: 26-33.

Dahlgren, P. 2009, Media and political engagement: citizens, communication, and democracy, Cambridge University Press, New York.

Di Pietro, Loredana and Eleonora Pantano. 2012. "An Empirical Investigation of Social Network Influence on Consumer Purchasing Decision: The Case of Facebook." Journal of Direct Data and Digital Marketing Practice 14: 18-29.

Ferguson, Rick. 2008. "Word of mouth and viral marketing: taking the temperature of the hottest trends in marketing." Journal of Consumer Marketing 25: 178-182.

Georgi, Dominik and Moritz Mink. 2012. "eCCIq: The

quality of electronic customer-to customer interaction," Journal of Retailing and Consumer Services http://dx.doi.org/10.1016/j.jretconser.2012.08.002.

Golan, Guy J. and Lior Zaidner. 2008. "Creative Strategies in Viral Advertising: An Application of Taylor's Six-Segment Message Strategy Wheel." Journal of Computer − Mediated Communications 13: 959-972.

Gonzalez, Cuitlahuac. 2010. "Social Media Best Practices for Communication Professionals through the Lens of the Fashion Industry." MA thesis, The University of Southern California.

Harris, Lisa and Charles Dennis. 2011. "Engaging customers on Facebook: Challenges for e-retailers," Journal of Consumer Behavior 10: 338-346.

Hartung, A. 2011. "Why Facebook beat MySpace," Forbes Online, viewed 26 September 2011, http://www.forbes.com/sites/adamhartung/2011/01/14/why-facebook-beat-myspace/

Hassanein, Khaled and Milena Head. 2005-6. "The Impact of Infusing Social Presence in the Web Interface: An Investigation across Product Types." Interactive Journal of Electronic Commerce 10: 31-55.

Heinonen, Kristina. 2011. "Consumer activity in social media: Managerial approaches to consumers' social media behavior." Journal of Consumer Behavior 10: 356-364.

Hill, Shawndra, Foster Provost, and Chirs Volinsky. 2006. "Network Based Marketing: Identifying Likely Adopters via Consumer Networks." Statistical Science 21: 256-276.

Hinchcliffe, D. 2006. "The State of Web 2.0", Web Services Journal, viewed 27 September 2011, http://web2.wsj2.com/the_state_of_web_20.htm

Hintz, A. 2007. "Civil society media at the WSIS: a new actor in global communication governance?" in B Cammaerts & N. Carpentier (eds), Reclaiming the media: communication rights and democratic media roles, Intellect Books, Bristol, pp. 243-264.

Hopper, P. 2007, Understanding cultural globalization,

Polity Press, Cambridge.

Jakubowicz, K. 2007. Rude awakening: social and media change in central and eastern Europe, Hampton Press, Cresskill.

Jenkins, H. Purushotma, R. Clinton, K. Weigel, M & Robison, AJ. 2005. Confronting the challenges of participatory culture: Media education for the 21st Century, viewed 20 September 2010, http://www.newmedialiteracies.org/files/working/NML WhitePaper.pdf

Kaplan, Andreas M. and Michael Haenlein. 2010. "Users of the World, Unite! The Challenges and Opportunities of social media." Business Horizons 53: 59-68.

Kelly, Louis, Gayle Kerr, and Judy Drennan. 2010. "Avoidance of Advertising in Social Networking Sites: The Teenage Perspective." Journal of Interacting Advertising 10: 16-27.

Mady, Tarek T. 2011. "Sentiment toward marketing: Should we care about consumer alienation and readiness to use technology?" Journal of Consumer Behavior 10: 192-204.

Mangold, Glynn W. and David J. Faulds. 2009. "Social Media: The New Hybrid Element of the Promotion Mix." Business Horizons 52: 357-365.

Muñiz, Albert M. and Hope Jensen Schau. 2007. "Vigilante Marketing and Consumer Created Communications." Journal of Advertising 36: 35-50.

Pavlou, Paul A. and David W. Stewart. 2000. "Measuring the Effects and Effectiveness of Interaction Advertising: A Research Agenda." Journal of Interactive Advertising 1: 62-78.

Pehlivan, Ekin, Funda Sarican, and Pierre Berthon. 2011. "Mining Messages: Exploring Consumer Response to Consumer vs. Firm Generated Ads." Journal of Consumer Behavior 10: 313-321.

Pookulangara, Sanjukta and Kristian Koesler. 2011. "Cultural Influence on Consumers' Usage of Social Networks and its' Impact on Online Purchase Intentions."

Journal of Retailing and Consumer Services 18: 348-354.

Shankar, Venkatesh, Jeffery Inman, Murali Mantrala, Eileen Kelley, and Ross Rizley. 2011.

Sinclaire, Jollean K. and Clinton E. Vogus. 2011. "Adoption of social networking sites: an exploratory adaptive structuration perspective for global organizations." Information Technology Management 12: 293-314, DOI 10.1007/s10799-011-0086-5.

Sorescu, Alina, Ruud T. Frambach, Jagdip Singh, Rangaswamy Arvind, and Cheryl Bridges. 2011. "Innovations in Retail Business Models."

Taylor, David G., David Strutton, and Kenneth Thompson. 2012. "Self-Enhancement as a Motivation for Sharing Online Advertising." Journal of Interactive Advertising 12:13-28.

Zeng, Fue, Li Huang and Wenyu Dou. 2009. "Social Factors in User Perceptions and Responses to Advertising in Online Social Networking Communities." Journal of Interactive Advertising 10: 1-13.

Zhang, Mimi, Bernard J. Jansen and Abdur Chowdhury. 2011. "Business engagement on Twitter: a path analysis." Electron Markets 21: 161-175. DOI 10.1007/s12525-011-0065-z.

Zinnbauer, Markus, and Tobias Honer. 2011. "How Brands Can Create Social Currency- a Framework for Managing Brands in a New Era." Marketing Review St. Gallen 28: 50-55.

OTHER BOOKS BY THE AUTHOR

Social Media Marketing 2023
https://www.amazon.com/dp/B0B4PGZ3DG/

Social Media Marketing 2023 (2 books in 1: *Social Media Marketing 2023* and *Social Media Marketing for beginners 2023*)
https://www.amazon.com/dp/B0BFP5L6MD/

Printed in Great Britain
by Amazon